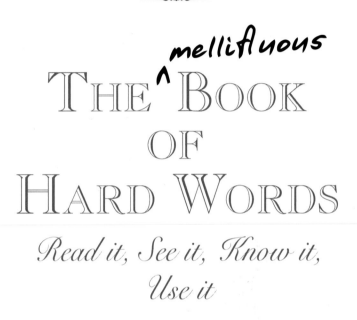

THE ^mellifluous BOOK
OF
HARD WORDS

Read it, See it, Know it,
Use it

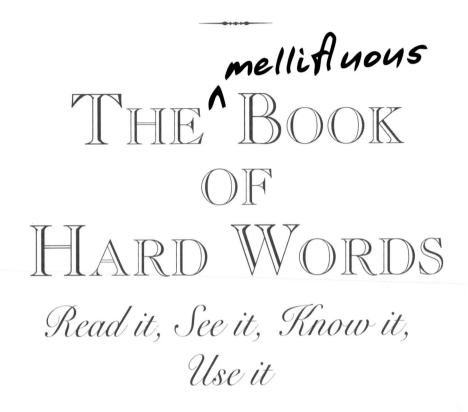

THE ^mellifluous BOOK OF HARD WORDS

Read it, See it, Know it, Use it

DAVID BRAMWELL

Crombie Jardine
Publishing Limited
Office 2
3 Edgar Buildings
George Street
Bath
BA1 2FJ

www.crombiejardine.com

This edition was first published by
Crombie Jardine Publishing Limited in 2008

ISBN 978-1-906051-23-5

This book was conceived, designed and produced by
iBall, an imprint of
Ivy Press
The Old Candlemakers
West Street, Lewes
East Sussex, BN7 2NZ
www.ivy-group.co.uk

Creative Director *Peter Bridgewater*
Publisher *Jason Hook*
Editorial Director *Caroline Earle*
Art Director *Sarah Howerd*
Senior Project Editor *Dominique Page*
Designer *Clare Barber*
Illustrator *Michael Chester*
Picture Researchers *Katie Greenwood, Sarah Skeate*
Concept *Viv Croot*

Printed in Thailand

CONTENTS

INTRODUCTION

This visual dictionary presents those words that we think we know, but don't really; the words we all use (sometimes), or listen to others use (more often), and wonder secretly what they actually mean. You can usually tell by the context, but it's easy to get it wrong. The Hard Words Read it-See it-Know it-Use it system is designed to banish all doubt. It's a simple programme. Each word is broken down into meaningful parts, then each part is illustrated, as is the whole word. Where relevant, we add the noun or adjective that goes with the main word, and bonus words that are related. Then we tell you where the word comes from, and finally how you can use it to upgrade your vocabulary.

This system can be applied to verbs, nouns (abstract and concrete) and adjectives because it works with the bricks and mortar that make up the word. Once you have learnt how a word is made and have pinned an image of it in your mind, you will never forget it. And the system will help you to look at other hard words fearlessly, break them down and tame them, then use them properly and effectively whenever you want to.

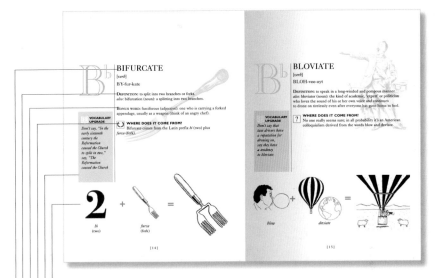

BIFURCATE
[verb]

BY-fur-kate

DEFINITION: to split into two branches or forks.
also: bifurcation (noun): a splitting into two branches.

BONUS WORD: furciferous (adjective): one who is carrying a forked appendage, usually as a weapon (think of an angry chef).

VOCABULARY UPGRADE
Don't say, "In the early sixteenth century the Reformation caused the Church to split in two," say, "The Reformation caused the Church

WHERE DOES IT COME FROM!
Bifurcate comes from the Latin prefix *bi* (two) plus *furca* (fork).

2 + *bi* (two) *furca* (fork) =

[14]

BLOVIATE
[verb]

BLOH-vee-ayt

DEFINITION: to speak in a long-winded and pompous manner.
also: bloviator (noun): the kind of academic, 'expert' or politician who loves the sound of his or her own voice and continues to drone on tirelessly even after everyone has gone home to bed.

VOCABULARY UPGRADE
Don't say that taxi drivers have a reputation for droning on, say they have a tendency to bloviate.

WHERE DOES IT COME FROM!
No one really seems sure; in all probability it's an American colloquialism derived from the words blow and deviate.

blow + *deviate* =

[15]

Illustration: images of each part of the word, making it easy to remember

Vocabulary upgrade: how to use the word, correctly in context

Where does it come from?: the language of origin is indicated by an icon

Extra information: a bonus word, an extension of the word or a useful word associated with it

Definition: what the word means in simple terms

Headword: the word, its grammatical identity and phonetic breakdown

WHERE DOES IT COME FROM?
A KEY TO THE ETYMOLOGY SYMBOLS

All words have an etymology, a provenance; they are usually based on words that come from old, often dead languages. For instant recognition, we use icons to indicate the source language of our hard words.

	American		Latin
	Chinese		Old German
	Greek		Old French
	Italian		Old Norse
	Japanese	**?**	Unknown

Androcentrism

Equipollent

Confabulate

Rodenticide

Hard Words

ANDROCENTRISM

[*noun*]

an-droh-SEN-tri-zum

DEFINITION: the practice of placing the male or man at the centre of one's view of the world.
also: androcentric (adjective): male-centred.

BONUS WORD: androcephalous (adjective): male-headed.

VOCABULARY UPGRADE

Don't say that Ancient Greece was a very masculine culture, say it was androcentric.

WHERE DOES IT COME FROM?
Androcentrism comes from the Greek prefix *andro* (male) plus *kentron* (centre).

andro
(male)

kentron
(centre)

ASTROBLEME

[*noun*]

AST-roh-bleem

DEFINITION: the mark left by a meteor. Literally a star-scar.

BONUS WORD: astrolatry (noun): star-worship.

WHERE DOES IT COME FROM?
Astrobleme comes from the Greek prefix *astro* (star) plus *blema* (wound).

VOCABULARY UPGRADE

Don't say the moon is full of craters from meteorites, say it is pitted with astroblemes.

astro
(star)

blema
(wound)

AUTODIDACT

[*noun*]

aw-toh-DIGH-dakt

DEFINITION: one who has never had, or has abandoned, formal education in favour of their own path of learning; a self-taught person. Famous autodidacts include Woody Allen, Bill Murray and Jane Austen.

also: autodidactic (adjective): self-teaching.

VOCABULARY UPGRADE

Don't say, "Did you know the author Maya Angelou never had a college education?"; say, "Maya Angelou is an autodidact."

WHERE DOES IT COME FROM?
Autodidact comes from the Greek prefix *autos* (self) plus *didaktos* (taught).

autos
(self)

+

didaktos
(taught)

=

BIBLIOMANIA
[*noun*]

bib-lee-oh-MAY-nee-uh

DEFINITION: a mania or obsession for collecting books. One notable celluloid bibliomaniac is Mel Gibson's character in the film *Conspiracy Theory*, who (for reasons we can leave to psychiatrists and conspiracy theorists) purchases a copy of the book *The Catcher in the Rye* every time he leaves his apartment.

also: bibliomaniacal (adjective): overzealous collecting of books.

BONUS WORD: biblioclast (noun): destroyer of books.

VOCABULARY UPGRADE

Don't say, "Do you think owning over a million books is a bit excessive?"; say, "Do you think it's a bit bibliomaniacal?"

WHERE DOES IT COME FROM?
Bibliomania comes from the Greek *biblion* (book) plus *mania* (madness).

biblion
(book)

mania
(madness)

[13]

BIFURCATE
[*verb*]

BY-fur-kate

DEFINITION: to split into two branches or forks.
also: bifurcation (noun): a splitting into two branches.

BONUS WORD: furciferous (adjective): one who is carrying a forked appendage, usually as a weapon (think of an angry chef).

VOCABULARY UPGRADE

Don't say, "In the early sixteenth century the Reformation caused the Church to split in two," say, "The Reformation caused the Church to bifurcate."

WHERE DOES IT COME FROM?
Bifurcate comes from the Latin prefix *bi* (two) plus *furca* (fork).

2   +   *bi* (two)   *furca* (fork)   =

BLOVIATE

[*verb*]

BLOH-vee-ayt

DEFINITION: to speak in a long-winded and pompous manner. *also:* bloviator (noun): the kind of academic, 'expert' or politician who loves the sound of his or her own voice and continues to drone on tirelessly even after everyone has gone home to bed.

VOCABULARY UPGRADE

Don't say that taxi drivers have a reputation for droning on, say they have a tendency to bloviate.

? WHERE DOES IT COME FROM?
No one really seems sure; in all probability it's an American colloquialism derived from the words blow and deviate.

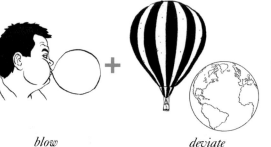

blow   *deviate*

CATALEPSY

[*noun*]

KAT-a-lep-see

DEFINITION: a state of complete immobility and rigidity in the human body.

BONUS WORD: cataplexy (noun): the same state, but in animals.

VOCABULARY UPGRADE

Don't say, "When I saw the yeti I was frozen with fear," say, "Upon seeing the yeti I entered a state of catalepsy."

WHERE DOES IT COME FROM?

Catalepsy is derived from the Greek *kata* (bearing down) plus the suffix lepsy from *lepsis* (seizure).

kata
(bearing down)

lepsis
(seizure)

C CONFABULATE

[*verb*]

kon-FAB-yoo-layt

DEFINITION: to confuse true and false memories.
also: confabulation (noun): a confusion of true and false memories.

📖 WHERE DOES IT COME FROM?
Confabulate comes from the Latin prefix *con* (with) plus *fabulari* (a made-up story).

📖 **VOCABULARY UPGRADE**

Don't say your grandmother's memory is confused, say she has a tendency to confabulate.

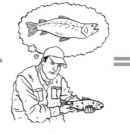

con
(with)

fabulari
(a made-up story)

C CONTRETEMPS

[*noun*]

KO(n)-trah-to(n)

DEFINITION: a mishap, an embarrassing incident or something occurring at exactly the wrong time.

 WHERE DOES IT COME FROM?
Contretemps comes from the Latin *contra* (against) plus *tempus* (time).

 **VOCABULARY UPGRADE**

Don't say that your trousers falling down during a job interview was a frightful embarrassment, say it was a contretemps.

contra
(against)

\+

tempus
(time)

\=

DISCOMBOBULATE

[*verb*]

dis-com-BOB-yoo-layt

DEFINITION: to upset or throw into disarray.

BONUS WORD: combobulate? Afraid not; this word has yet to exist.

? WHERE DOES IT COME FROM?

The word first came into existence around the mid-nineteenth century and is believed to be a bastardisation of discompose or discomfort. Like orange, there is no other word in the English language that rhymes perfectly with it.

📖 **VOCABULARY UPGRADE**

Don't say losing your blackberry has thrown your life into chaos, say it has discombobulated you.

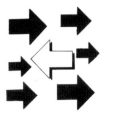

dis
(opposite)

compose

DOPPELGÄNGER

[*noun*]

DO-puhl-gang-uh

DEFINITION: a ghostly double of a living person, a look-alike or evil twin. Such apparitions are considered bad omens in folklore; the poet Percy Bysshe Shelley claimed to have dreamt about his doppelgänger shortly before he drowned.

 VOCABULARY UPGRADE

Don't say, "That ugly guy at work looks just like you," say, "He is your doppelgänger."

 WHERE DOES IT COME FROM?
Doppelgänger comes from the German *doppel* (double) and *gänger* (walker).

doppel
(double)

gänger
(walker)

EGREGIOUS

[*adjective*]

i-GREE-juhs

DEFINITION: outrageous, notorious, standing out from the crowd for all the wrong reasons. This word once meant "distinguished" but it is now derogatory.

VOCABULARY UPGRADE

Don't say, "attention-seeking fashion victim," say, "egregious personality."

WHERE DOES IT COME FROM?

Egregious comes from the Latin prefix *ex* or *e* (out of, away from) plus *grex* (flock). *Ex* takes the genitive form of the word *grex*, which is *gregis*, and the Latin word *egregius* means one who was chosen out of the flock.

ex
(out of, away from)

+

grex
(flock)

=

EQUIPOLLENT

[*adjective*]

e-kwi-POH-lent

DEFINITION: equal-powered or equal in force.

BONUS WORD: equiponderant (adjective): equal in weight.

WHERE DOES IT COME FROM?
Equipollent comes from the Latin *aequus* (equal) plus *pollentis* (strong).

VOCABULARY UPGRADE

If arm-wrestling matches with your grandma always come to a stalemate, don't say you are both as strong as each other, say you are equipollent.

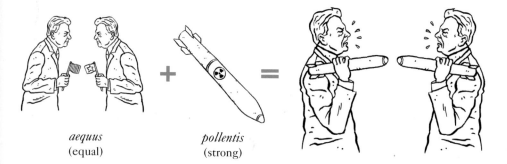

aequus
(equal)

pollentis
(strong)

ESPRIT DE CORPS

[*noun*]

es-pree-duh-KOR

DEFINITION: a common interest that unites a group of people; loyalty to a group or cause.

BONUS WORDS: esprit fort (noun): a free-thinker.

VOCABULARY UPGRADE

Don't say,
"We all became
friends through
our mutual
appreciation
of Tibetan nose
flute music," say,
"Tibetan nose flute
music was our
esprit de corps."

WHERE DOES IT COME FROM?
Esprit de corps comes from the French *esprit* (spirit, liveliness) plus *de corps* (of the body).

esprit
(spirit, liveliness)

de corps
(of the body)

EXCORIATE

[*verb*]

ek-SKOR-ee-ayt

DEFINITION: literally to strip the skin from; figuratively to criticise someone so harshly that they feel they have been flayed alive. *also:* excoriation (noun): severe criticism.

WHERE DOES IT COME FROM?
Excoriate comes from the Latin prefix *ex* (out of, away from), plus *corium* (animal hide or skin).

VOCABULARY UPGRADE

Don't say you're going to give your team the third degree when they lose again, say that you will excoriate them.

ex
(out of, away from)

corium
(animal hide or skin)

F f

FISSIPEDE

[*noun*]

FISS-ee-peed

DEFINITION: an animal with separate digits.

BONUS WORD: fissilingual (adjective): having a cloven tongue, such as found on a snake.

VOCABULARY UPGRADE

Don't say Homer Simpson has separate digits on his hand, say he is a fissipede.

WHERE DOES IT COME FROM?
Fissipede comes from the Latin *fissum* (to cleave or split) plus the suffix pede from *pedis* (foot).

fissum
(to cleave or split)

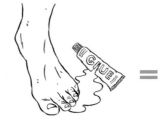

pedis
(foot)

F f

FUNAMBULIST

[*noun*]

fun-AM-bue-list

DEFINITION: a tightrope walker or rope dancer.
also: funambulate (verb): to walk or dance with ropes.

 **WHERE DOES IT COME FROM?**
Funambulist derives from the Latin *funis* (rope) plus *ambulare* (to walk).

VOCABULARY UPGRADE

Don't say, "Look at the funny man on the ropes, Mum," say, "Gosh, Mother, what a daring funambulist."

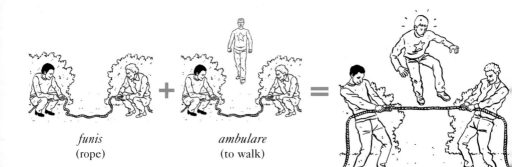

funis
(rope)

ambulare
(to walk)

GASTROMANCY

[*noun*]

GAS-troh-man-see

DEFINITION: attaining a connection with the divine through the use of guttural sounds in the belly or by gazing into belly-shaped glasses or bowls.

BONUS WORD: gastronome (noun): a lover of sensual delights, particularly food and wine.

VOCABULARY UPGRADE

Don't say Tibetan monks use deep-bellied singing to contact the divine, say they practise gastromancy.

WHERE DOES IT COME FROM?
Gastromancy comes from Greek and is made up of the prefix *gastero*, which derives from *gaster* (belly), and the suffix mancy from *manteia* (prophecy).

gaster
(belly)

manteia
(prophecy)

G  GENUFLECT

[*verb*]

JEN-yuh-flekt

DEFINITION: to bend at the knee in worship or reverence.
also: genuflection (noun): the act of bending the knee in worship.

WHERE DOES IT COME FROM?
Genuflect comes from the Latin *genu* (the knee) plus *flexum* (to bend).

 **+**  **=**

genu
(the knee)

flexum
(to bend)

HELIOTROPE

[*noun*]

HEE-lee-oh-trohp

DEFINITION: a plant whose flowers turn to face the sun.
also: heliotropic (adjective): sun-seeking (plant).

BONUS WORD: helioscope (noun): a telescope specially devised for observing the sun.

VOCABULARY UPGRADE

Don't say that your sunflowers turn toward the light, say they are heliotropes.

WHERE DOES IT COME FROM?
Heliotrope comes from the Greek prefix *helios* (the sun) plus the suffix *trope* (turning).

helios
(the sun)

trope
(turning)

HETEROGENEOUS

[*adjective*]

heh-teh-roh-JEN-nee-uhs

DEFINITION: different in kind; made up of different parts.

BONUS WORD: homogeneous (adjective): made up of the same parts.

VOCABULARY UPGRADE

Don't say London is home to a wide range of people from different backgrounds, say it has a heterogeneous population.

WHERE DOES IT COME FROM?

Heterogeneous comes from the Greek prefix *hetero* (other, different) plus the suffix geneous from *genos* (origin or birth).

hetero
(other, different)

genos
(origin or birth)

HYPERTROPHY

[*noun*]

high-PUHR-troh-fee

DEFINITION: abnormal enlargement, particularly of the human organs.
also: hypertrophic (adjective): pertaining to unusual enlargement.

WHERE DOES IT COME FROM?
Hypertrophic comes from the Greek prefix *hyper* (over) and the suffix *trophe* (nourishment).

VOCABULARY UPGRADE

Don't say, "I got into a brawl and ended up with a cauliflower ear," say, "I got into a brawl that left me with a hypertrophic ear."

hyper
(over)

+

trophe
(nourishment)

=

I i

IMPECUNIOUS

[*adjective*]

im-peh-KYOO-nee-uhs

DEFINITION: without, or short of, money.

BONUS WORD: impecuniosity (noun): the state of being without money.

VOCABULARY UPGRADE

Don't say, "I can't take you out for that slap-up meal; I'm flat broke," say, "I have to stay in bed tonight; I'm suffering from a touch of impecuniosity."

WHERE DOES IT COME FROM?
Impecunious comes from the Latin prefix *im* (without) plus *pecunia* (money).

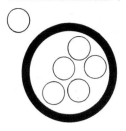

im
(without)

pecunia
(money)

I i

INVIOUS

[*adjective*]

IN-vee-uhs

DEFINITION: impassable; no way through.

WHERE DOES IT COME FROM?
Invious comes from the Latin prefix *in* (not) plus *via* (way).

VOCABULARY UPGRADE

Don't say, "It's too dangerous, Indiana; there is no way through these crocodile-infested swamps," say, "These are invious waters, Mr. Jones."

in
(not)

+

via
(way)

=

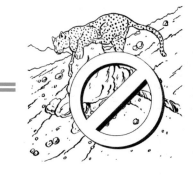

KOWTOW

[*verb*]

kow-TOW

DEFINITION: the act of protestation or bowing down, either in respect or hypocritically.

 WHERE DOES IT COME FROM?
Kowtow comes from the Chinese *k'o* (knock) and *t'ou* (head).

	VOCABULARY UPGRADE

Don't say, "I order you, my worthless minions, to bow down before me and kiss my feet," say, "I order you to kowtow."

+

=

k'o
(knock)

t'ou
(head)

LOGORRHEA

[*noun*]

log-oh-REE-uh

DEFINITION: excessive talking.

WHERE DOES IT COME FROM?

Logorrhea derives from the Greek *logos* (word) and *rhoia* (flow).

VOCABULARY UPGRADE

Don't say, "You talk too much," say, "You're suffering from logorrhea."

logos
(word)

rhoia
(flow)

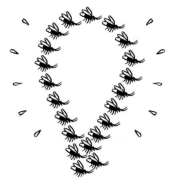

LUCIFEROUS

[*adjective*]

loo-SI-fuh-ruhs

DEFINITION: luminous, light-giving.
also: lucifer (noun): a match; the planet Venus as the morning star; and of course that old light-bringer, the Devil.

BONUS WORD: lucifuguous (adjective): shunning light.

VOCABULARY UPGRADE

Don't say that fireflies glow, say they have a luciferous quality.

WHERE DOES IT COME FROM?
Luciferous is derived from the Latin *lucis* (light) plus the suffix ferous from *ferre* (to bring).

lucis
(light)

+

ferre
(to bring)

=

MATROCLINOUS

[*adjective*]

ma-TROH-klin-uhs

DEFINITION: taking after one's mother; more like one's mother than one's father.
also: matrocliny (noun): the act of taking after one's mother.

 WHERE DOES IT COME FROM?
Matroclinous comes from the Latin *mater* (mother) plus the Greek *klinein* (to learn).

 VOCABULARY UPGRADE

Don't say, "You twiddle your hair like your mother," say, *"You have a matroclinous way of twiddling your hair."*

mater
(mother)

+

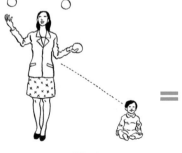

klinein
(to learn)

=

MELLIFLUOUS

[*adjective*]

mel-IF-floo-us

DEFINITION: (of sounds) sweetly smooth.
also: mellifluence (noun): a smooth, sweet flow.

BONUS WORD: mellification (noun): the production of honey.

VOCABULARY UPGRADE

Don't say that Paul McCartney's voice in The Beatles' song "Blackbird" sounds nice, say his voice is mellifluous.

WHERE DOES IT COME FROM?
Mellifluous derives from the Latin *mell* (honey) plus the suffix fluous from *fluere* (to flow).

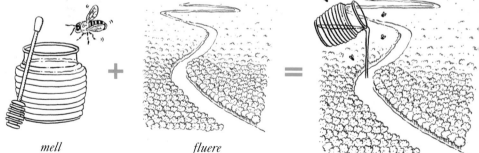

| *mell* | *fluere* |
| (honey) | (to flow) |

MONDEGREEN

[*noun*]

MOHN-deh-green

DEFINITION: a mishearing of a phrase, usually in a song, that creates a new meaning.

WHERE DOES IT COME FROM?

The word was coined by American writer Sylvia Wright in the 1950s on discovering that a line from a childhood song that her mother sang to her, "They have slain the Earl O'Murray and Lady Mondegreen," was actually, "They have slain the Earl O'Murray and laid him on the green!"

VOCABULARY UPGRADE

Don't say, "It's not 'the girl with colitis goes by,' it's 'the girl with kaleidoscope eyes!'" say, "My friend, that is a mondegreen."

Lady   Mondegreen

MOUNTEBANK

[*noun*]

MOWN-ti-bank

DEFINITION: a charlatan, quack or buffoon.
also: mountebankery (noun): the act of playing the role of charlatan.

WHERE DOES IT COME FROM?
Mountebank derives from the Italian *montare* (to mount) plus *banco* (bench).

VOCABULARY UPGRADE

Don't say your doctor is a quack, say he is a mountebank.

montare
(to mount)

banco
(bench)

NECROPOLIS

[*noun*]

neh-KROH-poh-lis

DEFINITION: cemetery.

BONUS WORDS: necromancer (noun): sorcerer; necrophagous (adjective): feeding off the dead.

VOCABULARY UPGRADE

Don't say you're heading down to the cemetery to visit your late Auntie Gladys, say you're visiting the necropolis.

WHERE DOES IT COME FROM?
Necropolis comes from the Greek prefix *necro* (dead) plus the suffix *polis* (city).

necro
(dead)

\+

polis
(city)

\=

O | ORTHOSTATIC

[*adjective*]

or-thoh-STA-tik

DEFINITION: standing erect.

BONUS WORD: orthoscopic (adjective): having 20/20 vision or a perfect panoramic view.

WHERE DOES IT COME FROM?

Orthostatic comes from the Greek prefix *ortho* (straight) plus the suffix static from *statos* (standing).

ortho
(straight)

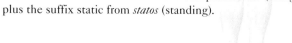

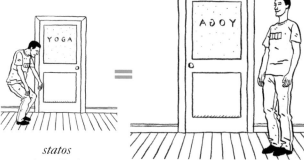

statos
(standing)

PERIPATETIC

[adjective]

per-i-pah-TEH-tik

DEFINITION: itinerant, wandering, walking about; the word is usually applied to a professional such as a teacher, who is employed by more than one establishment.

BONUS WORD: peripateticism (noun): the philosophy of Aristotle, who was said to teach while walking in the groves of the Lyceum in Athens.

VOCABULARY UPGRADE

Don't say he's an itchy-footed hobo afraid of commitment, say he is a peripatetic seeker of wisdom.

WHERE DOES IT COME FROM?
Peripatetic comes from the Greek prefix *peri* (around) plus patetic from the verb *pateein* (to walk); *peripatetos* is the Greek word for a stroll.

+

=

peri
(around)

pateein
(to walk)

PHANTASMAGORIA

[*noun*]

fan-taz-mah-GOR-ee-uh

DEFINITION: a series of illusory images or real forms that rapidly change in light and colour.
also: phantasmagorial (adjective): appearing to change rapidly in light and colour.

BONUS WORD: fantasmagoria (noun). Okay, this is not a bonus word, but an alternative spelling. Both versions can also be used to describe a French magic lantern show, which was popularised in the late eighteenth century.

WHERE DOES IT COME FROM?
Phantasmagoria derives from the Greek *phantasma* (an apparition) plus *agora* (a collection or group).

VOCABULARY UPGRADE

Don't say the Northern Lights look spooky, say they appear phantasmagorial.

phantasma
(an apparition)

agora
(a collection or group)

PLENILUNE

[*noun*]

PLEN-i-loon

DEFINITION: the full moon.
also: plenilunar (adjective): pertaining to a full moon.

BONUS WORD: plenipotence (noun): complete power.

VOCABULARY UPGRADE

Don't say, "Oh no, the full moon! I hope Tom doesn't turn into a werewolf again," say, "Oh no, it's the plenilune! I hope Tom doesn't have another attack of lycanthropy." (See page 79.)

WHERE DOES IT COME FROM?
Plenilune derives from the Latin *plenus* (full) and *luna* (moon).

+

=

plenus
(full)

luna
(moon)

PRETERNATURAL
[*noun*]

pree-tuhr-NA-chuh-ruhl

DEFINITION: supernatural, abnormal or not in accordance with nature.
also: preternaturalism (noun): belief in the supernatural.

VOCABULARY UPGRADE

Don't say you thought you saw a ghost, say you had a preternatural experience.

WHERE DOES IT COME FROM?
Preternatural derives from the Latin *praeter* (beyond) plus *natus* (to be born or be living).

praeter
(beyond)

natus
(to be born or be living)

R r° RHINOPLASTY

[*noun*]

RIGH-noh-plas-tee

DEFINITION: plastic surgery of the nose.

BONUS WORD: rhinorrhea (noun): excessive nasal mucus; rhinologist (noun): a nose specialist.

VOCABULARY UPGRADE

Don't say, "My God, what an ugly nose you have. You should get some surgery done on that monstrosity," say, "You need a spot of rhinoplasty, my friend."

WHERE DOES IT COME FROM?
Rhinoplasty comes from the Greek *rhinos* (nose) plus the suffix plasty from *plastikos* (to shape).

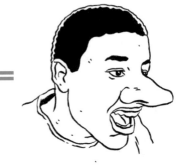

rhinos
(nose)

plastikos
(to shape)

R r RODENTICIDE

[*noun*]

roh-DEN-ti-sighd

DEFINITION: a poison for killing rodents.

WHERE DOES IT COME FROM?

Rodenticide comes from the Latin *rodens* (to gnaw) plus icide from the Latin *caedere* (to kill).

VOCABULARY UPGRADE

Don't say, "Those damned moles have been messing up my lawn again, I need to get rid of them," just rub your hands together and say, "It's time I bought some rodenticide."

+

=

rodens
(to gnaw)

caedere
(to kill)

SANGFROID

[*noun*]

SAH(ng)-FRWAH

DEFINITION: coolness or composure in the face of danger.

BONUS WORD: sang-de-boeuf (noun): a deep red, the colour of oxblood.

 VOCABULARY UPGRADE

Don't say that the English are courageous and face danger with a stiff upper lip, say they are a nation that excels in sangfroid.

WHERE DOES IT COME FROM?
Sangfroid comes from the French *sang* (blood) plus *froid* (cold).

sang
(blood)

\+

froid
(cold)

\=

SUBTERFUGE

[*noun*]

SUHB-tuhr-fyooj

DEFINITION: a trick or evasive device used for concealing something, often with regard to discussion.

BONUS WORD: subterhuman (noun): someone who is less than human.

 WHERE DOES IT COME FROM?
Subterfuge comes from the Latin *subter* (under) plus the suffix fuge from *fugere* (to take flight).

VOCABULARY UPGRADE

Don't say that politicians often wheedle their way out of difficult questions, say they apply subterfuge.

subter (under)	*fugere* (to take flight)	

TARDY-GAITED

[*adjective*]

TAR-dee-gay-tehd

DEFINITION: slow-paced.

BONUS WORD: tardive (adjective): late in development.

WHERE DOES IT COME FROM?
Tardy-gaited comes from the French *tard* (slow) plus *guêtre* (boot top, shoe).

VOCABULARY UPGRADE

Don't say, "I love my nine-inch high-heeled stilettos, but they do slow me down when I'm out walking," say, "My nine-inch stilettos make me tardy-gaited."

tard
(slow)

guêtre
(boot top, shoe)

THEOPHANY

[*noun*]

thee-O-fah-nee

DEFINITION: a vision of God.
also: theophanic (adjective): visionary.

BONUS WORD: theosophy (noun): divine or god-like wisdom.

 VOCABULARY UPGRADE

Don't say, "I had a vision of God in my tomato soup today," say, "I had a tomato-based theophany."

 WHERE DOES IT COME FROM?
Theophany comes from the Latin *theos* (God) plus the suffix phany from *phainein* (show).

theos
(God)

phainein
(show)

ULTRAMUNDANE

[*adjective*]

ul-tra-MUN-dayn

DEFINITION: beyond the world or physical limits.

BONUS WORD: ultramontane (adjective): beyond the mountains.

WHERE DOES IT COME FROM?

Ultramundane comes from the Latin *ultra* (beyond) plus *mundus* (the world).

VOCABULARY UPGRADE

If you had a dream that you were flying through the universe on a giant yogurt pot, don't say it was out of this world, say it was ultramundane.

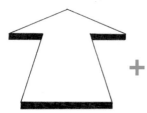

+

=

ultra
(beyond)

mundus
(the world)

WUNDERKIND

[noun]

VUHN-duhr-kint

DEFINITION: a child prodigy, someone who achieves incredible success at a very young age.

 WHERE DOES IT COME FROM?
Wunderkind comes from the German *wunder* (wonder) plus *kind* (child).

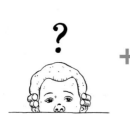 **VOCABULARY UPGRADE**

Don't say, "Well done, son, you have an incredible talent for the kazoo," say, "Son, you are a wunderkind!"

wunder (wonder)	*kind* (child)	

ZOOLITE

[*noun*]

ZOO-light

DEFINITION: a fossilised creature.

BONUS WORD: zoolatry (noun): the worship of animals.

WHERE DOES IT COME FROM?
Zoolite derives from the Greek *zoion* (animal) plus *ithos* (stone).

📖 **VOCABULARY UPGRADE**

Don't say you've found a pebble with a fossilised creature in it, say you've discovered a zoolite.

zoion
(animal)

ithos
(stone)

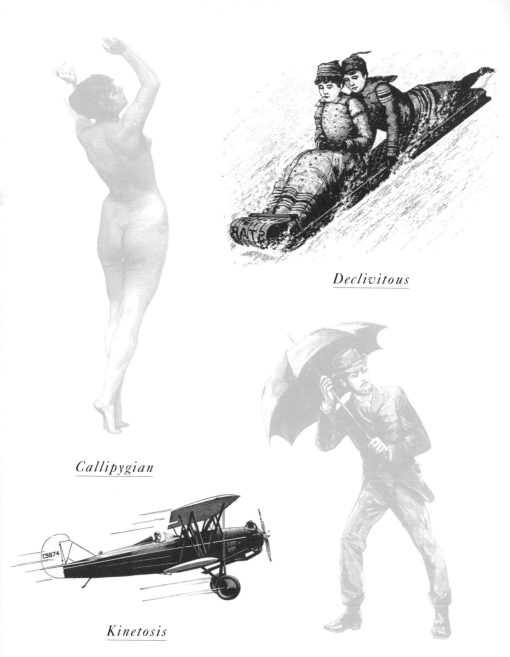

Declivitous

Callipygian

Kinetosis

Petrichor

HARDER WORDS

ACROHYPOTHERMIA

[*noun*]

a-kroh-high-puh-THUR-mee-uh

DEFINITION: abnormal coldness in the hands, feet and other bodily extremities.

WHERE DOES IT COME FROM?

Acrohypothermia comes from the Greek *akros* (highest, outermost) plus *hypo* (inadequate) and *therme* (heat).

VOCABULARY UPGRADE

If you climb into bed and your partner's feet are like ice, don't tell them they've got poor circulation, say they're suffering from acrohypothermia.

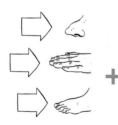

akros
(highest, outermost)

hypo, therme
(inadequate, heat)

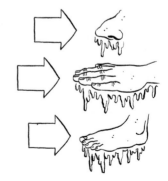

AILUROPHILE

[*noun*]

eye-LUHR-oh-file

DEFINITION: someone who loves cats, usually excessively or obsessively. The word was first recorded in 1927.
also: ailurophiliac (adjective): cat-loving; ailurophilia (noun): the love of cats.

BONUS WORD: ailurophobe (noun): someone who loathes and fears cats.

VOCABULARY UPGRADE

Don't say your uncle, who has 42 felines, is cat-crazy, say he is an ailurophile.

WHERE DOES IT COME FROM?
Ailurophile comes from the Greek *ailuros* (cat) plus the suffix phile from *phileein* (to love).

ailuros
(cat)

+

phileein
(to love)

=

ALEXIPHARMIC

[*adjective / noun*]

a-lekh-see-FAR-mik

DEFINITION: an antidote to poison.

WHERE DOES IT COME FROM?
Alexipharmic derives from the Greek *alexein* (to ward off) plus *pharmakon* (poison).

📖 **VOCABULARY UPGRADE**

If someone is suffering from a nasty snake-bite, don't say, "Looks like you require an antidote to the poison," say, "You are in urgent need of an alexipharmic."

alexein
(to ward off)

pharmakon
(poison)

BATHYKOLPIAN

[*adjective*]

ba-thi-KOHL-pee-an

DEFINITION: deep-bosomed.

WHERE DOES IT COME FROM?
Bathykolpian comes from the Greek *bathos* (deep) plus *kolpos* (cleft or gulf).

VOCABULARY UPGRADE

Don't say, "What ample dumplings you have, my dear wife," say, "What bathykolpian beauties you have been blessed with."

+

=

bathos
(deep)

kolpos
(cleft or gulf)

BELLES-LETTRES

[*noun*]

bel-LET-ruh

DEFINITION: elegant or fine writing. This term can refer to all forms in literature; it is often used in a modern sense with specific regard to essays, speeches, letters and humorous writing.
also: belletrist (noun): writer of elegant essays, speeches, etc.

VOCABULARY UPGRADE

Don't say he or she is an excellent writer of after-dinner speeches, say he or she is a belletrist.

 WHERE DOES IT COME FROM?
Belles-lettres comes from the French *belle* (beautiful) plus *lettres* (letters).

belle
(beautiful)

+

lettres
(letters)

=

CALLIPYGIAN

[*adjective*]

ka-lih-PI-ji-un

DEFINITION: possessing a fine pair of buttocks. Originally a description applied to Aphrodite as she arose from the foam, though this word is no longer gender-specific.
also: callipygous (adjective): fine-buttocked.

VOCABULARY UPGRADE

Don't say "J. Lo has got great buns," say, "She is extremely callipygian."

WHERE DOES IT COME FROM?
Callipygian comes from the Greek *kallos* (beautiful) plus *pyge* (buttocks).

kallos
(beautiful)

\+

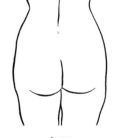

pyge
(buttocks)

\=

COPROLALIA

[*noun*]

koh-pro-LAH-lee-uh

DEFINITION: an involuntary or obsessive use of obscene language or words and phrases considered taboo.

BONUS WORD: coprophagist (noun): a person who eats dung.

 VOCABULARY UPGRADE

Don't say, "That comedian did nothing but swear all night on stage," say, "The comedian's performance was beset by coprolalia."

WHERE DOES IT COME FROM?
Coprolalia comes from the Greek *kopros* (dung) plus *lalia* (to talk).

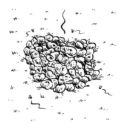

kopros
(dung)

lalia
(to talk)

DECLIVITOUS

[adjective]

deh-KLI-vih-tuhs

DEFINITION: downward-sloping, having a moderately steep incline.
also: declivity (noun): a place that slopes down or has an incline.

 WHERE DOES IT COME FROM?
Declivitous comes from the Latin prefix *de* (downwards) plus *clivus* (sloping).

 **VOCABULARY UPGRADE**

Don't say, "He has a very sloping nose," say, "His nose is particularly declivitous."

 +  =

de
(downwards)

clivus
(sloping)

DEFENESTRATION

[*noun*]

dee-fen-e-STRAY-shun

DEFINITION: a flinging of someone or something out of a window. *also:* defenestrate (verb): to fling something or someone from a window.

VOCABULARY UPGRADE

Don't say that all politicians should be thrown from a window, say they should be defenestrated.

WHERE DOES IT COME FROM?

Defenestration comes from the Latin prefix *de* (from, out of) plus *fenestra* (window). Historically, the word defenestration was used to refer to an act of political dissent and was coined in 1618 during the sacking of Prague Castle when a bunch of Catholics was thrown from its windows. Their subsequent survival was deemed "miraculous" by some; others prefer the story that they all landed in a big pile of horse manure.

de
(from, out of)

fenestra
(window)

DERMATOGLYPHICS

[*noun*]

duhr-mah-toh-GLI-fiks

DEFINITION: the science of the study of skin patterns such as fingerprints. Can also be used in reference to palmistry.

BONUS WORDS: dermal, dermic, dermatic (adjectives): consisting of skin.

VOCABULARY UPGRADE

Don't say that the police study fingerprints to catch criminals, say they practise dermatoglyphics.

WHERE DOES IT COME FROM?

Dermatoglyphics comes from the Greek *dermatos* (skin) plus the suffix glyphics from *glyphein* (to carve).

dermatos
(skin)

glyphein
(to carve)

ECHOPRAXIA

[*noun*]

e-koh-PRAK-see-uh

DEFINITION: the compulsion to repeat or imitate the movements and postures of those around one.

BONUS WORD: echolalia (noun): the involuntary repetition of another's words.

VOCABULARY UPGRADE

Don't say "Every time someone yawns I end up yawning too," say, "Yawning brings on a bout of echopraxia."

WHERE DOES IT COME FROM?
Echopraxia comes from the Greek *echo* (repeat) plus *praxia* (action).

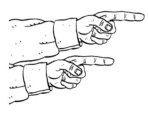

echo
(repeat)

praxia
(action)

EXTRAVASATE

[*verb*]

ex-TRAV-uh-sayt

DEFINITION: to force or pour out, particularly blood, lava or other viscous fluids.
also: extravasation (noun): fluids escaping from a living body or vessel.

VOCABULARY UPGRADE

Don't say, "Oh my Lord, the lava from that nearby volcano is pouring out; quick, everyone, run!" say, "Look, a volcanic extravasation... run like crazy!"

WHERE DOES IT COME FROM?
Extravasate comes from the Latin prefix *extra* (out of) plus *vas* (vessel).

extra
(out of)

vas
(vessel)

[69]

[IN] FLAGRANTE DELICTO

[*noun*]

fla-GRAN-tay deh-LIK-toh

DEFINITION: in the act of committing a crime. This term is most widely used nowadays to describe a couple caught in the act of sexual intercourse.

VOCABULARY UPGRADE

Don't say you were making mad, passionate love to your partner when your mother walked into the room, say you were caught in flagrante delicto.

WHERE DOES IT COME FROM?

In flagrante delicto comes from the Latin *flagrante* (burning) plus *delicto* (fault or crime) and literally translates as "while the crime is blazing."

flagrante
(burning)

delicto
(fault or crime)

GERONTOCRACY

[*noun*]

jer-on-TOH-krah-see

DEFINITION: a hierarchical institute run by an elder or elders. One notable example was the Soviet Union in the 1980s, during which time a string of decrepit septuagenarian leaders kept dropping like flies until the arrival of Mikhail Gorbachev.

BONUS WORD: gynocracy (noun): female-run government.

VOCABULARY UPGRADE

Don't say that this arm-wrestling society needs a leader with the wisdom of age and experience, say that this arm-wrestling society needs a gerontocracy.

WHERE DOES IT COME FROM?
Gerontocracy comes from the Greek *geron* (old man) plus *kratos* (strength).

geron
(old man)

+

kratos
(strength)

=

[71]

HIBERNACLE

[*noun*]

HY-buh-na-kuhl

DEFINITION: winter retreat.

BONUS WORD: hibernal (adjective): wintry.

VOCABULARY UPGRADE

Don't say that your hamster goes to sleep in its bed during winter, say it goes to its hibernacle.

WHERE DOES IT COME FROM?

Hibernacle comes from the Greek *hiberium* (winter) plus *taberna* (hut).

hiberium
(winter)

taberna
(hut)

HYPOGEUM

[*noun*]

hy-poh-JEE-uhm

DEFINITION: an underground chamber, vault or any part of a building set underground.

also: hypogeal (adjective): below ground.

BONUS WORD: hypogene (adjective): formed below the surface.

VOCABULARY UPGRADE

Don't say that Dracula sleeps in an underground chamber away from the light, say he sleeps in a hypogeum.

WHERE DOES IT COME FROM?

Hypogeum comes from the Greek prefix *hypo* (under) plus *gaia* (earth).

hypo
(under)

gaia
(earth)

 **I** i

IDIOGLOSSIA

[*noun*]

i-dee-oh-GLOH-see-uh

DEFINITION: a private language shared between children, particularly twins. It can also imply a situation in which a person's pronunciation is so bad as to render him or her unintelligible.

 WHERE DOES IT COME FROM?
Idioglossia comes from the Greek *idios* (own, private) plus *glossa* (tongue).

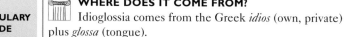 **VOCABULARY UPGRADE**

Don't say, "I can't understand a word you're saying with that cookie in your mouth," say, "A mouthful of cookies and you enter a state of idioglossia."

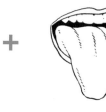

+

=

idios
(own, private)

glossa
(tongue)

I i

INTERCALATE

[*verb*]

in-TUHR-kah-layt

DEFINITION: to interpose or insert between – for example, the fitting of an extra day into a leap year.
also: intercalation (noun): an insertion.

VOCABULARY UPGRADE

Don't say that there is an extra day in February this year, say another day has been intercalated.

WHERE DOES IT COME FROM?

Intercalate comes from the Latin prefix *inter* (between) plus *calare* (to proclaim); the first of the month was always formally announced during Roman times.

inter
(between)

calare
(to proclaim)

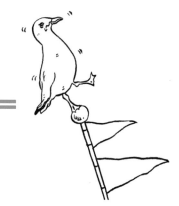

KINETOSIS

[*noun*]

ki-neh-TOH-sis

DEFINITION: motion sickness, usually brought on by cars, boats or planes.

BONUS WORDS: kinetic art (noun): any art in which movement plays a part, such as a wind sculpture.

VOCABULARY UPGRADE

Don't say after eating seven hamburgers, "This roller coaster is making me travel sick," say, "It is giving me kinetosis."

WHERE DOES IT COME FROM?
Kinetosis comes from the Greek *kinesis* (motion) plus *osis* (disease or illness).

kinesis
(motion)

osis
(disease or illness)

LALOPHOBIA

[*noun*]

lal-oh-FOH-bee-uh

DEFINITION: a morbid fear of speaking that is not just confined to public speaking, but exists in a wide variety of circumstances. *also:* lalophobic (noun): a person who fears speaking.

WHERE DOES IT COME FROM?

Lalophobia comes from the Greek *lalein* (to speak) plus *phobia* (fear).

VOCABULARY UPGRADE

Don't say that when it came to saying "I love you" you were unable to speak, say you were overcome with a bout of lalophobia.

lalein
(to speak)

+

phobia
(fear)

=

LEGERDEMAIN

[*noun*]

leh-jer-duh-MAHN

DEFINITION: sleight of hand; tricks.
also: legerdemain (adjective): trickery; juggling.

 WHERE DOES IT COME FROM?
Legerdemain derives from the French *léger* (light) plus *de main* (of the hand).

VOCABULARY UPGRADE

Don't say neat trick, say impressive legerdemain.

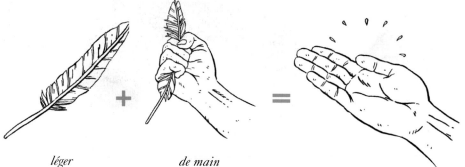

léger
(light)

de main
(of the hand)

LYCANTHROPE

[*noun*]

LIGH-kan-thrope

DEFINITION: a wolf-man or werewolf. The first recorded case in folklore of lycanthropy is Ovid's *Metamorphosis* in which Lycaon, the King of Arcadia, realising he's fresh out of beef, serves up his son as the main course after Zeus unexpectedly drops by for dinner. For his crime Lycaon is turned into a demented wolf.

also: lycanthropy (noun): the power of (or delusion of) transforming from man to wolf.

BONUS WORD: skiourosthropy (noun): the power to transform from man to squirrel.

WHERE DOES IT COME FROM?
Lycanthrope comes from the Greek *lykos* (wolf) plus *anthropos* (man).

VOCABULARY UPGRADE

Don't say your husband always gets more wolf-like around the full moon, say he gets a touch of lycanthropy.

lykos
(wolf)

anthropos
(man)

MAGNILOQUENT

[*adjective*]

mag-NI-loh-kwehnt

DEFINITION: to speak using high-flown or bombastic language. *also:* magniloquence (noun): speaking bombastically.

WHERE DOES IT COME FROM?
Magniloquent comes from the Latin *magnus* (great) plus *loqui* (to speak).

VOCABULARY UPGRADE

Don't say he uses too many big words when he speaks, say he speaks magniloquently (though of course this may be a case of the pot calling the kettle black).

magnus
(great)

loqui
(to speak)

NIDIFUGOUS

[*adjective*]

ni-DI-fue-jus

DEFINITION: nest-fleeing.

BONUS WORD: nidify (verb): to build a nest.

WHERE DOES IT COME FROM?

Nidifugous comes from the Latin *nidus* (nest) plus *fugere* (to flee).

VOCABULARY UPGRADE

Don't say, "Look Mum, the cute little birds are leaving their nest," say, "Look Mum, nidifugous fledglings."

nidus
(nest)

fugere
(to flee)

OENOPHILE

[*noun*]

EE-no-fy-uhl

DEFINITION: lover or connoisseur of wine.
also: oenophily (noun): knowledge of wines.

BONUS WORD: oenology (noun): the science of wine.

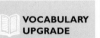
VOCABULARY UPGRADE

Don't say, "She certainly knows her wines," say, "She is an oenophile."

WHERE DOES IT COME FROM?
Oenophile comes from the Greek *oinos* (wine) plus the suffix *phile* (loving, attracted to).

oinos
(wine)

phile
(loving, attracted to)

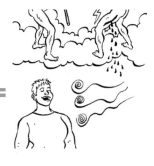

PETRICHOR

[*noun*]

PE-tri-kor

DEFINITION: the smell of rain after a period of dry weather.

WHERE DOES IT COME FROM?

Petrichor comes from the Greek *petri* (stone) plus *ichor* (the mineral said to be located in the blood of Greek gods). While the smell of fresh rain is often cited as many people's favourite odour, it wasn't until 1964 that anyone thought to give it a name. The word petrichor first appeared in *Nature* magazine and was coined by two Australian naturalists. The smell itself comes from the release (by fresh rain) of oils in certain plants that mix with minerals in the soil and stones.

VOCABULARY UPGRADE

Don't say, "I love the smell of rain that follows dry weather," say, "The fresh rain has brought a wonderful petrichor."

petri
(stone)

ichor
(mineral)

[83]

PROLICIDE

[*noun*]

PRO-li-syde

DEFINITION: the killing of offspring or an entire planetary race. *also:* prolicidal (adjective): having a predisposition to kill one's offspring.

VOCABULARY UPGRADE

Don't say you saw on a TV documentary that a desperately hungry mother rabbit will sometimes eat her young, say that she will sometimes resort to prolicide.

WHERE DOES IT COME FROM?
Prolicide comes from the Latin *proles* (offspring) plus *caedere* (to kill).

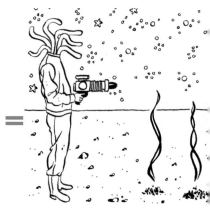

proles
(offspring)

caedere
(to kill)

P

PUSILLANIMOUS
[*adjective*]

pyoo-sil-AN-i-muhs

DEFINITION: feeble, lacking in determination, cowardly, mean-spirited, tiny-hearted.

WHERE DOES IT COME FROM?

Pusillanimous comes from the Latin *pusillus* (very small) plus *animus* (heart or spirit).

VOCABULARY UPGRADE

Don't say yellow-bellied chicken, say pusillanimous invertebrate.

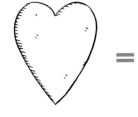

pusillus
(very small)

animus
(heart or spirit)

QUADRUMANE
[*noun*]

KWOD-ruh-mayn

DEFINITION: a creature capable of using all four feet as hands.
also: quadrumanous (adjective): four-handed.

WHERE DOES IT COME FROM?
Quadrumane comes from the Latin *quad* (four) plus
manus (hands).

VOCABULARY UPGRADE

Don't say a monkey can use its hands like feet, say it is a quadrumane.

quad
(four)

manus
(hands)

R^r RUBEFACTION

[*noun*]

roo-beh-FAK-shun

DEFINITION: reddening.
also: rubefy (verb): to make red, redden.

BONUS WORD: rubious (adjective): ruby or red-coloured.

VOCABULARY UPGRADE

Don't say the thought of kissing your lover makes your lips redden, say it makes them swell with rubefaction.

 WHERE DOES IT COME FROM?
Rubefaction comes from the Latin *rubeus* (red) plus *facere* (to make).

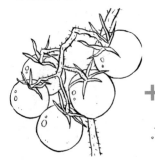

rubeus
(red)

facere
(to make)

SANSCULOTTE

[*noun*]

sanz-koo-LOT

DEFINITION: a revolutionary.
also: sansculottic (adjective): having revolutionary tendencies.

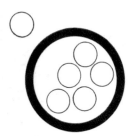
 WHERE DOES IT COME FROM?

Sansculotte comes from the French *sans* (without) plus *culotte* (knee-breeches). The term was first used during the French Revolution to describe the working-class extremists who wore full-length trousers rather than the fashionable knee-length culottes as favoured by the aristocracy. It may have been a term of derision, but it's fair to say the sansculottides had the last laugh.

sans
(without)

culotte
(knee-breeches)

S

SCHADENFREUDE

[*noun*]

SHAH-dun-froy-duh

DEFINITION: taking pleasure in another's misfortunes.

WHERE DOES IT COME FROM?
Schadenfreude comes from the German words *schade* (hurt) and *freude* (joy).

VOCABULARY UPGRADE

Don't say he takes great delight in watching others suffer, say he succumbs to schadenfreude.

   **+**

schade (hurt)	*freude* (joy)

S^S SUI GENERIS

[*noun*]

SOO-ee JEN-er-ihs

DEFINITION: unique; one-of-a-kind.

WHERE DOES IT COME FROM?
Sui generis comes from the Latin *sui* (him, her, it) plus *genus* (birth, species).

VOCABULARY UPGRADE

Don't say, "Hey, man, love your art, is it really painted entirely with bat-droppings? It's one of a kind!" say, "That's a sui generis work of art."

+

=
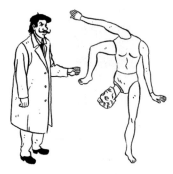

sui	*genus*
(him, her, it)	(birth, species)

TABULA RASA

[*noun*]

tab-u-la RA-sa

DEFINITION: a clean slate or a mind not yet influenced by external ideas and impressions.

WHERE DOES IT COME FROM?

Tabula rasa derives from the Latin *tabula* (writing tablet) plus *rasa* (clean).

VOCABULARY UPGRADE

Don't say that you believe we are born with no mental content, say you believe we are born with a tabula rasa.

tabula
(writing tablet)

rasa
(clean)

TERPSICHOREAN

[*adjective*]

turp-si-KOR-ree-uhn

DEFINITION: relating to dance and the enjoyment of it.
also: terpsichore (noun): the muse of song, dance and
body-popping.

WHERE DOES IT COME FROM?
Terpsichorean derives from the Greek *terpein* (to enjoy)
plus *choros* (dance).

VOCABULARY UPGRADE

*Don't say you
enjoy films that
are with or about
dancing, say you
enjoy films with
a terpsichorean
theme.*

+

=

terpein
(to enjoy)

choros
(dance)

THAUMATURGIST

[*noun*]

THOH-mah-tur-jist

DEFINITION: a wonder-worker or worker of miracles.
also: thaumaturgical (adjective): wonderful, magical (especially in relation to performance, legerdemain or work).

WHERE DOES IT COME FROM?
Thaumaturgist comes from the Greek *thaumatos* (miracle or magic) plus *ergon* (work).

📖 **VOCABULARY UPGRADE**

Don't say the author of this book has worked miracles, say he is a thaumaturgist!

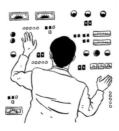

+

=

thaumatos
(miracle/magic)

ergon
(work)

VERISIMILITUDE
[*noun*]

ver-ih-sih-MI-lih-tyood

DEFINITION: the state or quality of something that resembles truth or reality.
also: verisimilar (adjective): truth-like. An example might be a piece of theatre or a film that appears to resemble reality.

 VOCABULARY UPGRADE

Don't say the new Bond film is unrealistic, say it lacks verisimilitude.

WHERE DOES IT COME FROM?
Verisimilitude comes from the Latin *verus* (truth or reality) plus *similus* (like).

verus
(truth or reality)

similus
(like)

VITUPERATE

[*verb*]

vi-TOO-puh-rayt

DEFINITION: to criticise using abusive language.
also: vituperation (noun): abuse.

WHERE DOES IT COME FROM?
Vituperate comes from the Latin *vitium* (a fault) plus *parare* (to prepare).

VOCABULARY UPGRADE

Don't say, "How dare you yell at the kids, they didn't mean to scratch your new car," say, "How dare you vituperate."

vitium
(a fault)

parare
(to prepare)

WELTSCHMERZ

[*noun*]

VELT-shmerts

DEFINITION: a melancholia towards the state of the whole world; a pessimistic world view.

WHERE DOES IT COME FROM?
Weltschmerz comes from the German *welt* (world) plus *schmerz* (pain).

VOCABULARY UPGRADE

Don't say, "I'm feeling depressed at the state of the world," say, "I'm developing weltschmerz."

welt
(world)

+

schmerz
(pain)

=

XENOGENESIS

[*noun*]

zen-oh-JEN-e-sis

DEFINITION: the creation of offspring with biological characteristics totally different to those of their parents.

BONUS WORD: xenogeneous (adjective): due to outside influence.

VOCABULARY UPGRADE

Don't say you can't understand how your child has ended up with a dome-shaped head and tentacles, say you think an act of xenogenesis has taken place.

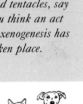 **WHERE DOES IT COME FROM?**
Xenogenesis comes from the Latin prefix *xeno* (foreign, strange) plus *genesis* (birth, creation).

xeno
(foreign, strange)

genesis
(birth, creation)

Nychthemeron

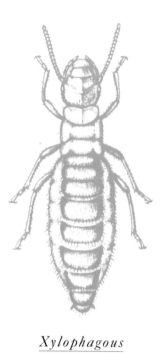

Xylophagous

Concupiscence

Obstreperous

HARDEST WORDS

AGAMOGENESIS

[*noun*]

a-GA-moh-JEN-e-sis

DEFINITION: reproduction without the union of parents of different sexes.
also: gamogenesis (noun): sexual reproduction.

 WHERE DOES IT COME FROM?
Agamogenesis comes from the Greek prefix *a* (non) plus *gamos* (sexual union) and *genesis* (beginning, creation).

VOCABULARY UPGRADE

Don't say, "Did you know that a female turkey can produce fertilised eggs in the absence of a male?" say, "Did you know a female turkey is capable of agamogenesis?"

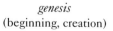

a, gamos
(non, sexual union)

genesis
(beginning, creation)

ANTHROPOPHAGOUS

[*adjective*]

an-throh-POH-fah-guhs

DEFINITION: man-eating.

also: anthropophagi (noun, plural): man-eaters. It is also the name of headless creatures from English folklore with eyes in their shoulders, mouths in their chests and brains in their genitals.

VOCABULARY UPGRADE

Don't say, "I'm so hungry I could eat my own arm," say, "I'm so hungry it's giving me anthropophagous thoughts."

WHERE DOES IT COME FROM?

Anthropophagous comes from the Greek prefix *anthropos* (human) plus *phagein* (to eat).

anthropos
(human)

phagein
(to eat)

BOUSTROPHEDON

[*adjective*]

boo-STROH-feh-dohn

DEFINITION: alternating from right to left and left to right, particularly with regard to the reading or writing of a text in which the lines are read in opposite directions.

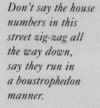

VOCABULARY UPGRADE

Don't say the house numbers in this street zig-zag all the way down, say they run in a boustrophedon manner.

WHERE DOES IT COME FROM?

Boustrophedon comes from the Greek *bous* (ox) plus *strophe* (turning).

bous
(ox)

strophe
(turning)

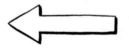

CONCUPISCENCE

[*noun*]

kon-KYU-pih-sehn(t)s

DEFINITION: intense desire or lust.
also: concupiscent (adjective): lustful.

WHERE DOES IT COME FROM?

Concupiscence comes from the Latin prefix *con* (with or together) plus *cupere* (to desire).

VOCABULARY UPGRADE

Don't say, "My heart yearns for you, I feel a stirring in my loins," say, "You fill me with concupiscence."

 +  =

con
(with or together)

cupere
(to desire)

DOLICHOCEPHALIC

[*adjective*]

doh-li-koh-seh-FAH-lik

DEFINITION: long-headed.
also: dolichocephal (noun): long-headed person.

WHERE DOES IT COME FROM?
Dolichocephalic comes from the Greek prefix *dolicho* (long) plus *kephale* (head).

VOCABULARY UPGRADE

Don't say that anteaters have long heads, say they are dolichocephalic.

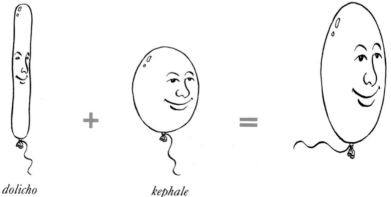

dolicho
(long)

kephale
(head)

F f FLOCCINAUCINIHILI-PILIFICATION

[*noun*]

FLOK-in-OH-sin-i-HIL-i-PIL-i-fi-KAY-shun

DEFINITION: the act of considering something of little or no value. Logoleptics might enjoy knowing that it is the longest word in this book and exactly two letters longer than honorificabilitudinitatibus (deserving respect or love), the longest word found in Shakespearean prose. It is not, however, as long as pneumonoultramicroscopicsilicovolcanoconiosis, alleged to be one of the longest words in the dictionary. Okay, enough silliness.

VOCABULARY UPGRADE

Don't say that your partner doesn't give you the respect you deserve, say their attitude toward you is one of floccinaucinihilipilification.

WHERE DOES IT COME FROM?

Floccinaucinihilipilification comes from the Latin *floccinauci* (in an instant), *nihil* (nothing), *pili* (a hair) plus *facere* (to do).

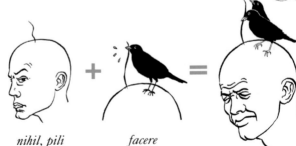

floccinauci
(in an instant)

nihil, pili
(nothing, a hair)

facere
(to do)

HIPPOCREPIAN

[*adjective*]

hip-oh-**KREH**-pee-an

DEFINITION: shaped like a horseshoe.

 WHERE DOES IT COME FROM?
Hippocrepian comes from the Greek *hippos* (horse) plus *krepis* (shoe).

VOCABULARY UPGRADE

Don't say the street your mad aunt lives on is horse-shoe-shaped, say it is hippocrepian.

 **+**  **=**

hippos
(horse)

krepis
(shoe)

IGNIS FATUUS

[*noun*]

IG-nis FA-chuh-wuhs

DEFINITION: a fluorescent light that hovers over damp marshy ground or bogs at night and seems to move away as the observer gets closer; a deluded idea that leads one astray.
also: other words and phrases for this phenomenon include will-o'-the-wisp, jack-o'-lantern, corpses' candles and friar's lantern.

VOCABULARY UPGRADE

Don't say your grandfather's dream of being an acrobat seems a trifle deluded, say it is ignis fatuus; a will-o'-the-wisp.

WHERE DOES IT COME FROM?

Ignis fatuus comes from the Latin *ignis* (fire) plus *fatuus* (foolish). The name will-o'-the-wisp comes from several British folk tales that usually involve the Devil and a mischievous character called Will, who lures unwary travellers to their watery graves with embers or hot coals provided by Old Nick.

ignis
(fire)

+

fatuus
(foolish)

=

I i

INTERNUNCIO

[*noun*]

in-tuhr-NUHN-see-oh

DEFINITION: a messenger between two parties.

WHERE DOES IT COME FROM?
Internuncio comes from the Latin *inter* (between) plus *nuncios* (messenger).

inter
(between)

nuncios
(messenger)

KAKEMONO

[*noun*]

kak-i-MOH-noh

DEFINITION: mounted Japanese scroll wall painting.

 WHERE DOES IT COME FROM?
Kakemono comes from the Japanese *kake* (to hang) plus *mono* (thing).

kake
(to hang)

mono
(thing)

LEPTODACTYLOUS

[*adjective*]

lep-toh-DAK-ti-luhs

DEFINITION: slender-fingered or toed.
also: leptodactyl (noun): a creature with slender toes.

BONUS WORD: leptosome (noun): slender-bodied person.

 VOCABULARY UPGRADE

Don't say, "Ooh, haven't you got lovely slim fingers," say, "Your leptodactylous beauty thrills me."

WHERE DOES IT COME FROM?
Leptodactylous comes from the Greek *lepton* (slender) plus *daktylos* (digit).

+

=

lepton
(slender)

daktylos
(digit)

LISSOTRICHOUS

L

[*adjective*]

li-SOH-tri-kuhs

DEFINITION: smooth- or straight-haired.

WHERE DOES IT COME FROM?
Lissotrichous comes from the Greek *lissos* (smooth) plus *trichos* (hair).

VOCABULARY UPGRADE

Don't say your girlfriend has lovely smooth hair on her face, say that she has a lissotrichous face.

lissos
(smooth)

trichos
(hair)

METEMPSYCHOSIS

[*noun*]

meh-tem-sy-KOH-sihs

DEFINITION: the migration of the soul after death and its reincarnation in another body. Metempsychosis is a popular belief in both Hindu religion and Klingon. In fact without it a certain pointy-eared hero would never have been brought back from the dead in *Star Trek III: The Search for Spock.*

VOCABULARY UPGRADE

Don't say, "I believe when I die I will return as a little tortoise called Trevor," say, "Metempsychosis will result in my returning as Trevor the tortoise."

WHERE DOES IT COME FROM?

Metempsychosis comes from the Greek prefix *meta* (beyond) plus *psyche* (the soul).

meta
(beyond)

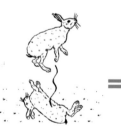

psyche
(the soul)

NYCHTHEMERON

[*noun*]

nik-THEM-ur-on

DEFINITION: a 24-hour period, night and day.
also: nychthemeral (adjective): 24-hourly.

BONUS WORD: nyctalopia (noun): night-blindness.

VOCABULARY UPGRADE

Don't say you're going to a party for 24 hours, say you're planning a nychthemeral party.

WHERE DOES IT COME FROM?
Nychthemeron comes from the Greek *nyktos* (night) plus *hemera* (day).

+

nyktos
(night)

hemera
(day)

=

OBSTREPEROUS

[*adjective*]

ob-STRE-puh-ruhs

DEFINITION: noisy, clamorous; making a loud noise.
also: obstreperousness (noun): an unruly and noisy manner.

 WHERE DOES IT COME FROM?

Obstreperous comes from the Latin prefix *ob* (against, before) plus streperous from the Greek *strepere* (to make a noise).

 VOCABULARY UPGRADE

If you've sold your children to medical science and need to break it to your partner, don't say, "Honey, they were just getting far too noisy and unruly," say, "Honey, they were getting way too obstreperous."

ob
(against, before)

strepere
(to make a noise)

P P POCOCURANTE

[*adjective / noun*]

poh-koh-kyoo-RAN-teh

DEFINITION: indifferent, nonchalant; uncaring. An uncaring person. *also:* pococuranteism (noun): the act of being uncaring.

 WHERE DOES IT COME FROM?
Pococurante comes from the Italian *poco* (a little) plus *curante* (to care).

VOCABULARY UPGRADE

Don't say he or she cares little for others, say he or she is pococurante.

poco
(a little)

curante
(to care)

Q | QUAQUAVERSAL

[*adjective*]

kwa-kwa-VUHR-suhl

DEFINITION: going off in all directions at once or facing all ways.

WHERE DOES IT COME FROM?
Quaquaversal comes from the Latin *quaqua* (every which way) plus *versum* (to turn).

VOCABULARY UPGRADE

Don't say when you're nervous your thoughts become scattered, say they become quaquaversal.

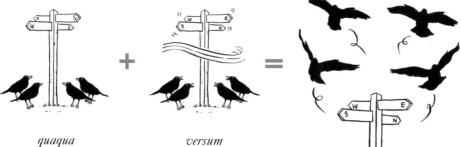

quaqua
(every which way)

versum
(to turn)

RECALCITRATE

[*verb*]

ri-KAL-si-trayt

DEFINITION: to be opposed to something.
also: recalcitrant (adjective/noun): opposing, a stubborn opponent;
recalcitrance (noun): strong objection or opposition.

VOCABULARY UPGRADE

Don't say that whenever you try to get your husband to eat his peas he gets annoyed and throws them at you, say he becomes recalcitrant.

WHERE DOES IT COME FROM?
Recalcitrate comes from the Latin prefix *re* (repeat, again) plus *calcis* (heel).

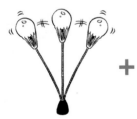 **+** 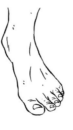 **=**

re
(repeat, again)

calcis
(heel)

SANGUISUGENT

[*adjective*]

san-gwih-SOO-jent

DEFINITION: bloodthirsty.

BONUS WORD: sanguinolent (adjective): bloody.

 **WHERE DOES IT COME FROM?**
Sanguisugent comes from the Latin *sanguis* (blood) plus *siccus* (thirsty).

 VOCABULARY UPGRADE

Don't say the Vikings were a bloodthirsty race, say they were sanguisugent.

+

=

sanguis
(blood)

siccus
(thirsty)

SESQUIPEDALIAN

[*adjective / noun*]

ses-kwih-puh-DAY-lee-yuhn

DEFINITION: using words with many syllables (often in a pedantic or smug manner); a very long word.

BONUS WORD: sesquialtera (noun): a perfect fifth in music.

VOCABULARY UPGRADE

Don't say, "I'm not just using overly long words to try and impress you," say, "There's nothing sesquipedalian about me."

WHERE DOES IT COME FROM?
Sesquipedalian comes from the Latin *sesqui* (half) plus *pedis* (foot); literally meaning written words that are a foot and a half in length!

sesqui
(half)

pedis
(foot)

TATTERDEMALION

[*noun / adjective*]

ta-tuhr-deh-MAY-lee-on

DEFINITION: a person dressed in ragged or torn clothes. Ragged in appearance or being in a decayed state. Tatterdemalion is also the name of a *Marvel Comics* supervillain, noted for his hobo-like appearance and unsociable habit of secreting a noxious chemical that can burn through paper.

VOCABULARY UPGRADE

Don't say, "Urgh! What a scruffy tramp," say, "There goes a right tatterdemalion!"

 WHERE DOES IT COME FROM?
Tatterdemalion comes from the Old Norse *tattur* (rags) plus the French *maillon* (long clothing).

tattur
(rags)

+

maillon
(long clothing)

=

TRANSPONTINE

[adjective / noun]

trans-PON-teen

DEFINITION: across a bridge, situated on the south side of the Thames River in London; melodramatic (owing to the style of theatre once performed south of the River Thames).

WHERE DOES IT COME FROM?

Transpontine derives from the Latin *trans* (across) plus *pons* (bridge). The word pons gave rise to the Indo-European root *pent*, leading to the French *pont* (bridge) and Russian *sputnik* (travelling companion).

trans
(across)

pons
(bridge)

TRISKAIDEKAPHOBIA

[*noun*]

tris-ky-dek-ah-FOH-bee-uh

DEFINITION: unreasoning superstitious fear of the number 13, a number regarded with apprehension in many cultures. *also:* triskaidekaphobic (adjective).

WHERE DOES IT COME FROM?
Triskaidekaphobia comes from the Greek *tris* (three), *kai* (plus), *deka* (ten) and *phobia* (fear).

 VOCABULARY UPGRADE

Don't say you're scared witless by the number 13, say you suffer from triskaidekaphobia.

tris, kai, deka
(three, plus, ten)

 +

phobia
(fear)

=

ULOTRICHY

[*noun*]

yoo-LOH-tri-kee

DEFINITION: excessively curly- or woolly-hairedness.
also: ulotrichous (adjective): belonging to a woolly-haired group.

WHERE DOES IT COME FROM?
Ulotrichous comes from the Greek *oulos* (woolly) plus *trix* (hair).

 VOCABULARY UPGRADE

Don't say you can never get a comb through your hair in the morning because it's so thick, say you are a victim of ulotrichy.

oulos
(woolly)

trix
(hair)

VENTRIPOTENT

[*adjective*]

ven-TRI-poh-tent

DEFINITION: with great appetite and capacity.

WHERE DOES IT COME FROM?
Ventripotent comes from the Latin *venter* (belly) plus *potens* (powerful).

VOCABULARY UPGRADE

Don't say you're feeling really hungry, say you're feeling ventripotent.

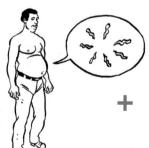

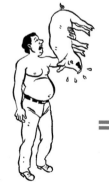

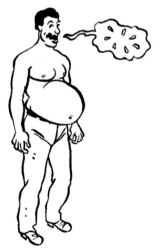

venter
(belly)

potens
(powerful)

XYLOPHAGOUS

[*adjective*]

zigh-LOH-fah-gus

DEFINITION: wood-eating.

BONUS WORD: xylophilous (adjective): fond of wood, living on wood.

VOCABULARY UPGRADE

Don't say, "My mother's mahogany leg has been ruined by wood-eating termites," say, "My mother's mahogany leg has been devoured by xylophagous termites."

WHERE DOES IT COME FROM?
Xylophagous comes from the Greek *xylon* (wood) plus *phage* (to eat).

\+

=

xylon
(wood)

phage
(to eat)

INDEX